101

Quips *and* Quotes

for Tweens, Teens and Twenties to win with

ADA ADELEKE-KELANI

AuthorHouse™
1663 Liberty Drive
Bloomington, IN 47403
www.authorhouse.com
Phone: 833-262-8899

Because of the dynamic nature of the Internet, any web addresses or links contained in this book may have changed since publication and may no longer be valid. The views expressed in this work are solely those of the author and do not necessarily reflect the views of the publisher, and the publisher hereby disclaims any responsibility for them.

Any people depicted in stock imagery provided by Getty Images are models, and such images are being used for illustrative purposes only.
Certain stock imagery © Getty Images.

This book is printed on acid-free paper.

ISBN: 978-1-6655-1175-9 (sc)
ISBN: 978-1-6655-1174-2 (e)

Library of Congress Control Number: 2020925675

Print information available on the last page.

Published by AuthorHouse 03/12/2021

authorHOUSE

Contents

Gift page

To:

_____

Message:

_____

_____

_____

From:

_____

Dedication

To God, Who blessed my husband and I with our sons,
Obasegun and Ibunkunolu, who are blessings in every way.

This book is also dedicated to our sons –
from whom we have learned a lot and continue to learn from.

And of course, dedicated to my lifelong learning partner – 'Leke.

Acknowledgement

This book had been in the making and only made it to the top of the list after one of my cousins heard about my books. After hearing about my books and watching some of the videos on my YouTube channel: *'Quip Corner with Ada'*, she asked, "Do you have something for teenagers?" It immediately stoked the fire in me. Prior to that conversation, at least one other person had asked me the same question especially as they had initially assumed that my first book: *"101 Quips and Quotes that will charge and change your life"* was a children's book. So, I kept the questions on the back burner of my mind.

Later, I mentioned the questions to my friend, Dr Chinyere Almona, an author herself. She "kindly" responded "maybe you should." And "should" I have done. So Chidi Essell, thank you for being one of the catalysts for this book and Chi, thank you for your unwavering support, including being my alpha reader.

I cannot but also acknowledge and thank my husband, Leke, for his steadfast support. Among many other contributions, he chose the "author picture" on the back cover. He is my love for life, lifelong learning partner and partner in parenting our winsome sons.

I am of course grateful for and to our sons, Obasegun and Ibunkunolu. Oba, as usual, helped me decide on and "design" the book cover. Ibunkun was my "Writing Coach"; he insisted that I read and re-read my manuscript out loud to him and challenged me to think through what I really meant by each one. Thank you, sons.

I also acknowledge all of you my readers – including all you adults who were once tweens, teens and may still be in your twenties. And of course, I acknowledge all you parents too. Thank you all for reading and doing your part to win and help others win in life.

Introduction

Guess what? When I started on this book project, I did not have a title, so I initially saved my manuscript as "Book Y". As the book project progressed, one day it occurred to me that "Book Y" was an apt, though temporary, title – simply because of how many times we ask "Why?" as children, tweens, teens and twenties – and even as adults.

Knowing why is critical and central to our living our best lives which is why it is equally important to ask the right people those questions (pun intended). This book has the answers to some of the "Why?" questions I had when I was in my tweens, teens and twenties and to the same and other "Why?" and "But, why?" questions from my sons and others in those age ranges.

When I mentioned this book idea to my sons saying that I would need them to please review the manuscript (beta readers), one of them said, "Oh like Chicken Soup for the Soul?" then quickly added, "Just don't sound like a parent". So, I located and elevated my inner child, who "came", faced challenges, and conquered in her tweens, teens, twenties and is now an adult (and gratefully, a parent).😊

Tweens, Teens and Twenties, I am hopeful that by the time you (your family members and your friends) finish reading this book you will know that being you is the best thing you can do for yourself and for the rest of the world that you are here to impact positively. And remember that the last letter in the word "Why" is the first letter in the word "You". Know your WHY and simply be yourself because you are YOUnique.

Love and Hugs
Auntie Ada

Chapter 1

Go with God

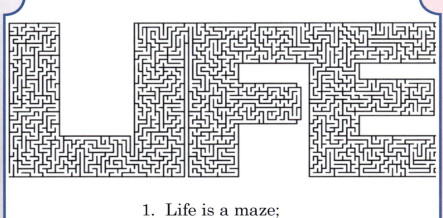

1. Life is a maze;
walking with God makes it amazing.

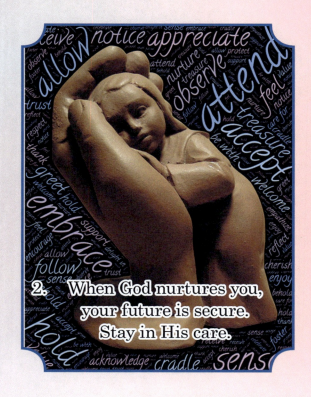

2. When God nurtures you,
your future is secure.
Stay in His care.

3.   God has your best interest at heart,
it is in your best interest to stay connected to Him.

4.   Those who do not hallow God, have and live hollow lives.

5.   Overconfidence is always misplaced except when placed in God.

6.   The most important thing about doing God's will is doing it
His way, not your way.

7.   Approval from people is a nice-to-have
but God's approval is a need-to-have.
Focus on what you need to have, and you will get all you need.

8.   Things may not always be great, but we can choose to always be
grateful to God.

Chapter 2

Family matters

9.   Your family's support can also be
your shelter;
just as God is our support and shelter.

10.   Your parents
are always
there to
watch your back.

11. Parents always have your best interest at heart
— even when they are pushing you.

12. (Much as you may wish) your parents'
love for you is not blind.
They see and know you with all your flaws
and still see you as "flawesome."

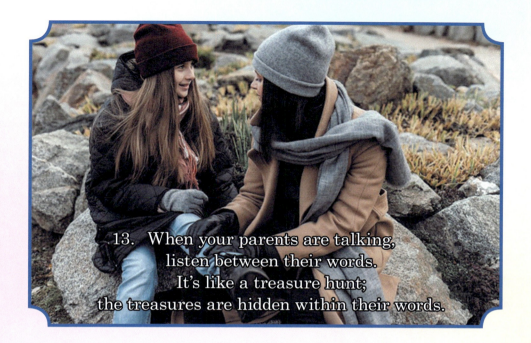

13. When your parents are talking,
listen between their words.
It's like a treasure hunt;
the treasures are hidden within their words.

14. Parents do not always say
all that they mean,
but they mean all that they say.

15. Parents have an interestingly
"annoying" way of showing their love.
The important thing is that their love is
always genuine when it is shown.

16. Talk to and confide in your parents.
Your secrets are safest with them.
As you may know,
they know more about you than you know.

17. Knowing how happy your parents
     were when you were born should
     motivate you to keep them happy.

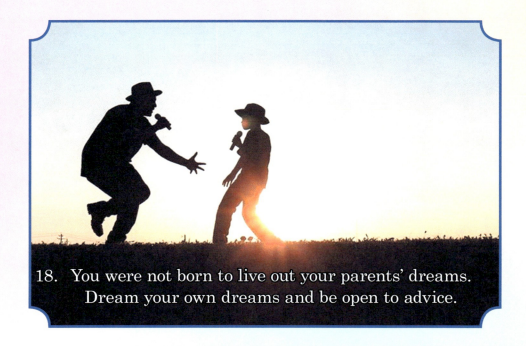

18. You were not born to live out your parents' dreams.
     Dream your own dreams and be open to advice.

19. Some of our older relatives
show us what is possible —
and motivate us to reach for
our own goals.

20. Being more enlightened than your
parents and grandparents will never make
you more experienced than they are —
take advantage of their experience.

Chapter 3

Friendship

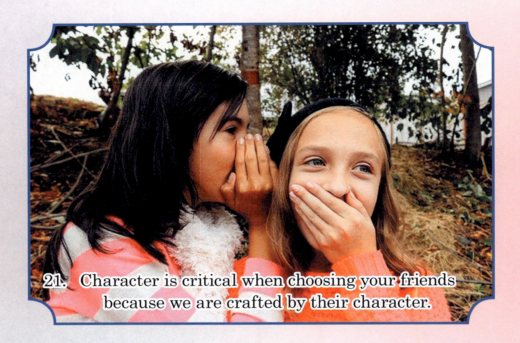

21. Character is critical when choosing your friends because we are crafted by their character.

22. If you hang out with the wrong people, they will hang you out to dry when you need them to help you.

23. Ensure that you are not befriending people
you should be defriending and vice versa
because it will impact how things end up for you.

24. Take care that the people you mingle with do not mangle you.

25. Good friends help you by hindering you from
going down the wrong paths.
Bad friends hinder you by helping you go down the wrong paths.

26. Your life will never be like your friends' lives because
you are not your friends – you are you for a reason.
Make your life the best possible one.

27. If you try to be everything to everyone,
you will be no one to yourself.

28. No matter how fond you become of your friend,
fondling should not be part of your friendship.

29. There are some friends you need to let go of
so you can grow and glow
because they are in the way of your flow.

30. The quality of friends you have
is more important than
the quantity of friends you have.

Chapter 4

Be yourself

31. Do not lose yourself trying to fit in with others.
Stand out – you are YOUnique.

32. You were born
beautiful
now it's up to you to
live a beautiful life
every day.

33. You don't have to always
"colour within the lines"
- be and express your authentic self.

34. Your attitude is within your control.
Control your attitude because
it controls everything else.

35. Your attitude to life determines life's response to you.

36. Trying to look and sound cool could make you show up as uncouth.

37. Don't keep doing things you don't like because you want people to like you otherwise soon, you won't like yourself.

38. Do not let your voice get lost in the world's noise.

39. It is always easier to be you...
otherwise you'll waste valuable time practising
to be someone else.

40. Do not look down on anyone,
because they may be the ones who help you up in future.

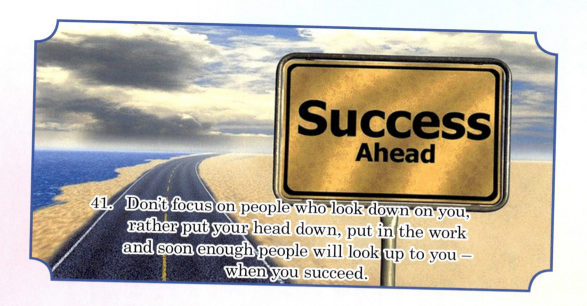

41. Don't focus on people who look down on you, rather put your head down, put in the work and soon enough people will look up to you — when you succeed.

42. Choosing to stretch yourself is choosing to overcome and achieve more in life.

43. You are born to do great things, so, dig in your heels and deepen your roots so you can grow and stand tall.

44. Give your best to life and life will give you the best.

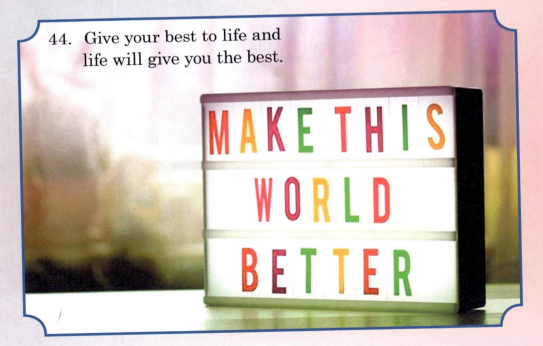

Chapter 5

Lean-in to learn

what **?** where
how why
when who

45. A questioning mind is a growing mind,
just make sure you are asking the right people.

46. Asking for advice is a sign of wisdom —
just like someone who is lost asking for directions.

47. Sometimes the only way you get to know what you don't know is by asking someone who knows more than you know.

48. It is always safer to ask questions than to guess the answer – and get it wrong.

49. It is wise to learn from your mistakes and
foolish to want to be left alone to make all the mistakes
possible.

50. One bad mistake when you make a mistake,
is not learning from the initial mistake.

51. Learn to learn from what people say about you
– and get better not bitter.

52. What you earn in future is dependent on what you learn
each day.

53. There's a place for fresh ideas and a place for time-tested ones.
Maturity is knowing which place you are in.

54. Look and learn then leverage what you have learned
and leap forward.

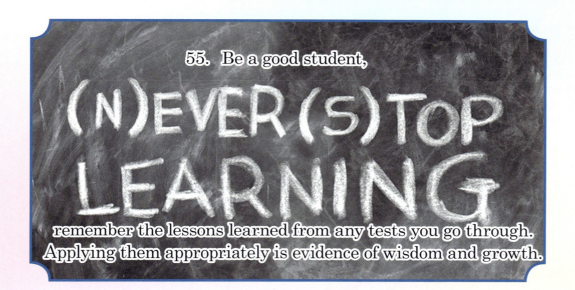

55. Be a good student,

(N)EVER (S)TOP LEARNING

remember the lessons learned from any tests you go through.
Applying them appropriately is evidence of wisdom and growth.

56. There is always more to what you look at
than what you see.
Learn to look beyond the obvious.

(For instance, what do you see in this picture?
The answer is at the end of the book).

Chapter 6

Self-management

Downloading Future
Please Wait...

57.   Do not be in a hurry to become an adult.
It will come with time and then
you will be one for the rest of your life.

Cancel

58.   Growing old is outside your control...
only growing up is within your control.

59. Wishing that you are an adult sooner may result in
you missing out on your younger years.

60. Going slowly is better than not going at all.
Growing slowly is better than not growing at all.

61. Learn to enjoy moments and have memories rather than
spending those moments only taking pictures.

62. Flattery flattens; it can lead you to falter and fail…
don't fall for it.

63. If you lose sight of what is right,
you will end up right in the middle of what is wrong.

64. The easiest way to know the right way to go is by not always
following the crowd.

65. If you make others look small so you look big and better, you will never grow because you are focusing on making others look worse rather than working on bettering yourself.

66. Only get into positions, pictures, and places that you won't mind seeing in online posts and other spaces.

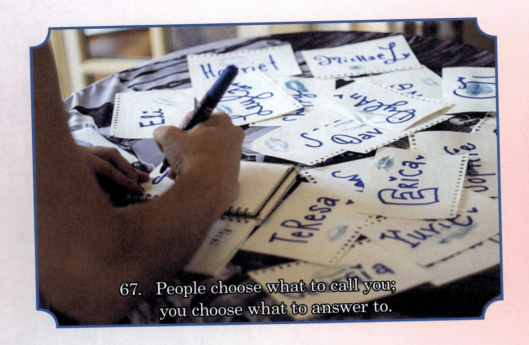

67. People choose what to call you;
you choose what to answer to.

68. When you learn to enjoy your own company,
other people are likely to also enjoy your company.

69. What people say about and to you is not as important as
what you say about and to yourself.
No one can love you more than you love yourself.

70. Mind your mind; do your best with all your mind and strength.

71. Your strength of character inside helps you withstand
whatever is outside.

72. Do not get so caught up highlighting what has gone wrong
that you miss out celebrating all that has gone right.

73. Your morality could impact your mortality (and your eternity).
Good morals underpin a good life – here and hereafter.

74. If a caterpillar does not follow the right process,
it will never become a butterfly.
To fulfill your purpose, you need to know
and follow the right process.

75. Do not give up...
if you do not persist and come out of your cocoon
you may die without ever flying.

76. Don't quit - just fit or refit yourself with grit
and keep moving forward.

77. Your words create your world –
choose your words carefully.

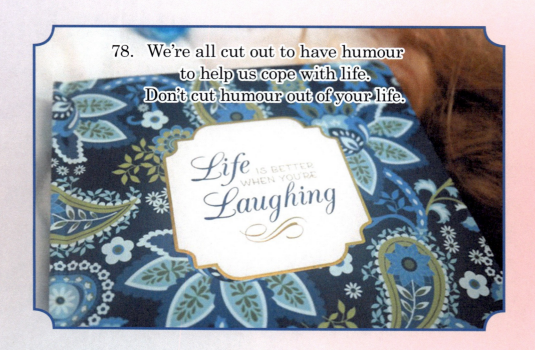

78. We're all cut out to have humour
to help us cope with life.
Don't cut humour out of your life.

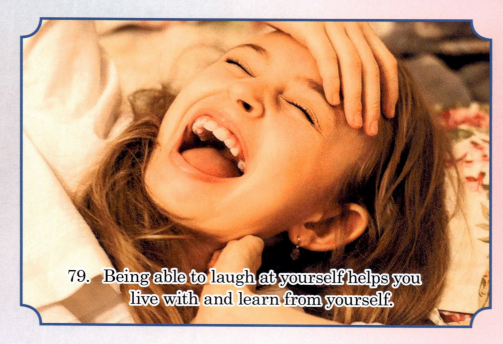

79. Being able to laugh at yourself helps you
live with and learn from yourself.

Chapter 7
Live future-focussed

80. You may not be sure about your future career,
just be sure about getting an education —
it's the foundation you can build on.

81. The more you read, the more you grow
and are better equipped to lead.

82. Your future is bright, and it starts now - so focus on doing the right things starting right now.

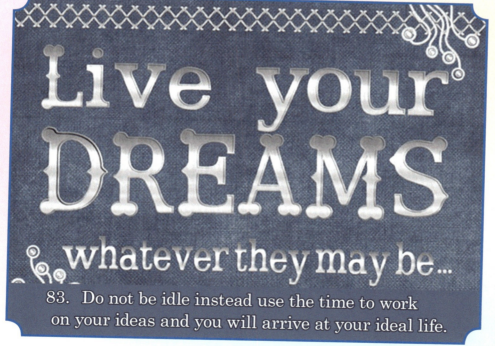

Live your DREAMS whatever they may be...

83. Do not be idle instead use the time to work on your ideas and you will arrive at your ideal life.

84. You cannot hold time back so
get on with what you need to do.
Now is the time to act.

85. Do not lose sight of your (childhood) dreams –
at the right time they will come true.

Chapter 8

Make impact

86. Your footprints in the sands of time
should be as unique as your fingerprints.

87. Remember that no matter how much
you have accomplished,
there is still a lot more that you can accomplish.

88. Your youthfulness should not limit your usefulness.

89. Do what you can today so that tomorrow you are not regretting what you did not do yesterday. Your future is only a day away.

90. What you do or do not do today determines
what you will have or not have tomorrow.

91. It's your life so motivate yourself.
Don't wait for others to motivate you...it's your life.

92. "It's my life" is a true statement.
Just remember that your life affects others.

93. You may not be able do all things well,
so do the things you can really well.

94. Sometimes you should do what you can do otherwise
you would regret not doing what you should have done
when you could have done it.

95. When you think deeply, you will be able to connect the dots
and see the picture your life is creating.

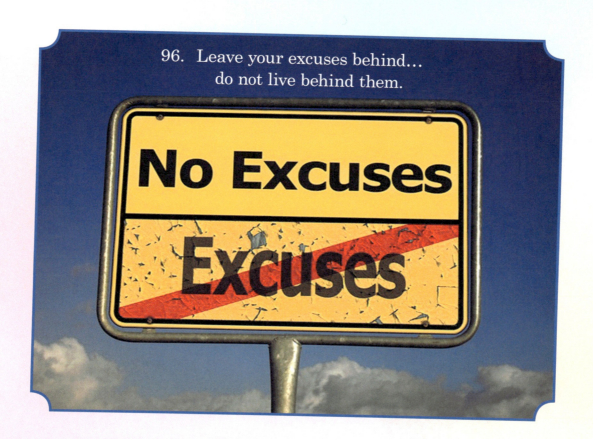

96. Leave your excuses behind...
do not live behind them.

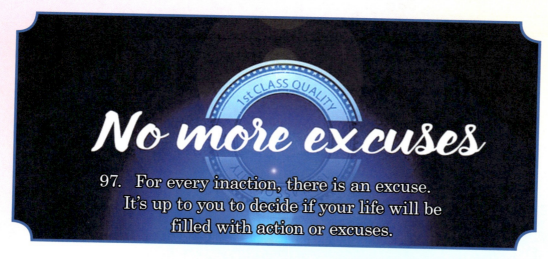

No more excuses

97. For every inaction, there is an excuse.
It's up to you to decide if your life will be
filled with action or excuses.

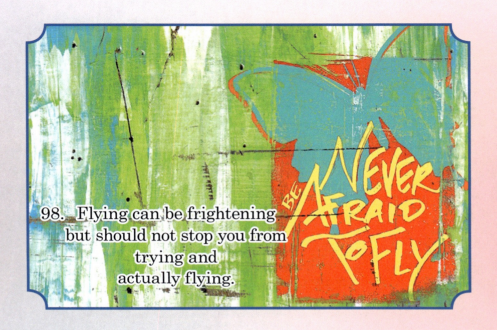

98.   Flying can be frightening but should not stop you from trying and actually flying.

99.   Everyone you meet has "wings" and you can be the "wind" that makes them lift upward or makes them drift away.

100. Do not lose sight of the "why" – having the right "why" behind every "what" you want to do will help you know the right who, when, where and how to do it.

101. The value you add to the world is sometimes seen one petal at a time.

From my budding kwip kings

1. Make little goals so you can achieve your big goals.
   – Oba Adeleke

2. Know how you learn, then you'll learn much quicker.
   – Oba Adeleke

3. Don't be socially awkward; have forward energy and make friends.
   – Oba Adeleke

4. If people put a label on you, they are just labels, and they can be removed.
   – Oba Adeleke

5. When you take your mind off what's bothering you,
   your mood improves.
   – Oba Adeleke

6. The person who knows that they do not know is better than
   the person who does not know that they do not know.
   – Ibunkun Adeleke

7. Life is tough - don't make it tougher.
   – Ibunkun Adeleke

8. The first step to solving a problem is knowing that there is one.
   – Ibunkun Adeleke

9. Be NICE – noble, integrous, considerate, empathetic.
   – Ibunkun Adeleke

My aha! moments

Quip number   Quip-spiration

_____   _____

_____   _____

_____   _____

_____   _____

_____   _____

_____   _____

_____   _____

_____   _____

_____   _____

_____   _____

_____   _____

_____   _____

_____   _____

Conclusion

After writing my second book titled: ***"101 Quips and Quotes that will strengthen and sweeten your marriage and family relationships***", I felt it would be complementary to write a book for the younger generation. And writing this book was interesting and almost intimidating.

First, I had to think back to how I felt and what I experienced when I was in my tweens, teens and twenties. Then I compared that to my experience as a mother of children currently in two of those age ranges.

My main challenge was to identify the similarities and differences between both periods – mine and theirs and share tips, written as quips and quotes, that helped me, helps them and continues to help others win in life.

As I wrote this book, one thing that came through is that in life, there is always more to what we look at than what we see after our first look. Therefore, it is important that in all our interactions, we take time to look, take in what we see – and possibly do something about what we notice, as necessary.

By the way, the answer to the question added to Quip 56 is:
It is a picture of a vase (black) and outlines of the side
view of two heads (white). Take another look.

I am very hopeful that this book has helped you see and do more in your life and the lives of those around you, including:
- 🏆 **W**illingness to learn, relearn and sometimes unlearn,
- 🏆 **I**ntentionality in your decisions and actions, and
- 🏆 **N**urturing the right relationships – first with yourself and then with others.

Keep winning in life!

Other books in the 101 Quips and Quotes Book Collection

Autographed copies of all my books can be obtained using this link:
https://101quipsandquotes.blogspot.com/

Email: DiamondCutterCoach@outlook.com

Printed in the United States
by Baker & Taylor Publisher Services